ALL THINGS SANE

T.S. WOLFF

Print ISBN: 979-8-9906587-0-7

E-Book ISBN: 979-8-9906587-1-4

Editor: Meg Ryan

Book Design by Nuno Moreira, NMDESIGN

ALL
THINGS
SANE

T.S. WOLFF

A STORY OF LOVE GONE WRONG
— TOLD IN POEMS

CONTENTS

For J, because I love/d you
and one time you made me promise
I would dedicate something to you.

PROLOGUE

Once, when I was a child
before I had a woman's body
someone, somewhere
a man
I can't remember who
looked me up and down
and said

someday
you are going to make
someone
very happy.

And I
believed him.

1

Before love I slept.
After love I never slept again.

THE BEGINNING

First day of a new job. Sophomore year of college. Lincoln, Nebraska.

I find him in a cubicle. Jeans,
Birkenstocks.   Thin frame
kicked back in an office chair,
hands behind his head, elbows out.

When he sees me, his eyebrows arch.
He leans forward and extends his hand.
His palm is smooth and cool.
Ash brown hair falls in pieces.

Outside, wind pushes snow
into corners. Frost fogs
all the windows. The office wraps
around us like a cocoon.

The edge of his jaw is strong.
I like the pressure of his grip.
But when he stands up, I see he is scrawny
and not much taller than me.

I give him a smile, then turn
and continue down the hall.
I ride an elevator to a basement
lined with shelves.

Files in cabinets covered in dust.
Stacks of boxes to be packed and labeled.
The records will be ordered by number.
The fluorescent lights hum.

On my way out, he stands smoking
in the building's entrance, hiding
from the cold. He is almost right
but not exactly right.

Like a lighter flicked and then gone out.
My eye caught for a moment only.

THE LIBRARIAN

He leads me through the office, where books
lie in stacks on desks, and files half-fill boxes.
He smells good, I think as we wander the rows.
His t-shirt is soft, the hem of his jeans frayed just so.

Scientific data, he explains, turning to face me.
We will compile the critical information
into a master list. He presses his finger
against his thumb and stabs the air.

We will organize everything
into a standard system. We will create
the most efficient bureaucratic science library
in the history of bureaucratic science libraries.

I look at him sideways and squint.
He picks up a clipboard, shows me
the work already accomplished
the details pinned on paper.

He shuffles through a stack of files.
You should read some of this if you get a chance.
It's a great opportunity to learn
about the resources of Nebraska.

He shrugs. *If you're into that*
sort of thing. Most people aren't.
Most people don't read.
They know nothing about science.

He has been looking at me longer
than most people look at each other.
It probably sounds nerdy, he says,
and twists a piece of hair.

I shake my head.
I try to hide a smile.
This scrawny boy in this strange library.
This smell of musty paper and cologne.

IN THE BASEMENT

I glance up from my filing to find him
half hidden in the shelves.
He grins at me, then vanishes
down a row.

When he reappears, he suggests
we file together. So we clear off a desk.
He writes labels with the energy of progress.
In his wake the numbers assume an attitude of confidence.

He says as a child he wandered farmland.
He says his parents are poor.
He says he used to believe in God
but now he doesn't.

He wants to force himself to consider
ideas other than the ones he was raised with.
He doesn't want to get stuck
being a boy from small town Nebraska.

From his words I can tell he has read a lot of books.
He wields speech like a carving tool,
cuts jokes so tight, other people don't notice them.
When our eyes meet, we both laugh silently.

One day he asks me what kind of music I like
and the next day he plays a CD by that band.
Often he says the idea in my mind before I can say it.
Or else he says an idea I would never imagine on my own.

He gives me a book by Charles Bukowski.
He gives me music by Wilco and Modest Mouse.
He considers me across the desk. Tell me, he says,
what qualities you want most in a man.

My stomach clenches.
Kindness, I tell him.

IN THE LAST ROW OF SHELVES

He demands to know
if the Bukowski poems offend me.
I say they do not,
although privately I wonder
if he chases women with the coldness
Bukowski does.
I wonder if he uses women
as a means to expand his mind.

He demands I name my favorite tracks
on the Wilco album.
When I list my favorite tracks,
he widens his eyes and nods.
He says the tracks I like
are, in fact, the best ones.

He studies my face
as if we were old friends
who haven't seen each other
in decades.

In the last row of shelves we stand
close to each other. His head inclines
in my direction. He smells like the sea
and something warm and drifting.

I start to think the most fun thing
would be to put my mouth
over his mouth.
But I do not.

A S A T U R D A Y I N F E B R U A R Y

Cold weather and gray skies
have always been things to endure.
But this afternoon it's cozy to hide inside,
dreamy to be in the kitchen making enchiladas.
When J arrives, the apartment smells like peppers.
We eat and slouch and watch movies.
I imagine I feel his eyes on me.
I arrange my hair to fall at a pretty angle.
We discuss plants and art and God.
I say I am not sure what I believe about religion,
but I would like to find out if it is true.
He says I look too innocent
to be smoking a blunt.
Usually I try to minimize
the things about me that seem innocent,
but I'm willing to let him
see me that way if he wants to.
When he stands to leave,
the afternoon falls back into the ordinary.
On his way out, he offers
to move a coffee table for me
from the living room to the hallway.

THEOLOGIANS

Theologians don't know nothing
about my soul
— Wilco

My favorite Wilco album is *A Ghost Is Born*.
J likes *Yankee Hotel Foxtrot*.
But on *A Ghost Is Born*, we both like
track #10 best.

The melody dances, showing off.
The drums desire the keyboard
and the keyboard agrees.
An electric guitar pleads.
In the thick of it all, Jeff Tweedy's voice curls
like smoke in a closed room.

The lyrics work like medicine.
They raise the feeling
that is missing from religion.
They remind us truth exists.
They whisper to the part
inside each of us that is lonely.

We listen to this song over and over.
We love it the same amount.
We let the music make
something beautiful between us.

The part in me that is lonely
takes a deep
breath in.

FIRST NIGHT TOGETHER

I have heard that he might have a girlfriend
but he doesn't mention her to me.

I have not spent time with very many boys.
I feel tense and uncertain.

But then, one afternoon,
he looks at me with so much light in his eyes
that when everyone else climbs out of his car,
I stay.

We watch movies at his house until the sun is gone.
The small space between us whispers a question.

After a while he rests his head on my shoulder.
Later, I find his bedroom walls are painted green.

I look up at the ceiling in the almost-darkness.
I say I can't have sex with him.
I am a virgin, and I might
save myself for marriage.

He says this is ok.
He asks if I trust him.
I pause.
Yes, I say.

HOW THE SILENCE STARTS

Later we discuss the situation.
I ask if he has a girlfriend.
He says he does.

We agree we shouldn't complicate work.
We decide we should just be friends.
There are rules about these things,
we know.

I ask if he will tell his girlfriend about me.
He says he will if it comes up.

My heart sinks, but I nod anyway.
I have no materials to build an argument.

I think I can control myself.
I guess nothing fun is sane.

FRIENDS

So we stay out of bedrooms.
We work.
We talk.
We read.
We get high.
We drive around.
Sometimes we don't need
to talk.

I follow him to lovely places.
We listen to jazz at coffee shops.
We lounge in living rooms
that look like dusty pieces of art.
We drive gravel roads
he's known since childhood.
The scenes are illuminated by a type of light
that makes everything else diminish.

I know he tells me more things
than he tells anyone else.
I know he doesn't deceive me.
I know the person you deceive the least
is the person you love the most.

I like to remember the certainty of his hands on me.
I like to watch him flick cigarettes.
I like to see him press his forefinger against his thumb
when he is making a point.

H O W I K N O W

I know because he looks me in the eyes
and tilts his head to the left, slowly.
I know because he speaks so softly
I have to move closer to hear him.
I know because he follows me down hallways
and forgets where he was going.

I start thinking about strange things.
I think about the night my father came
to my mother and planted me there inside her.
I think about the moment before he quite reaches her,
the moment when I am at the very brink
between being and not being.

In that imagining, I see something pawing
at the veil that is the world.
I see what happens when what could be
breaks the last holding
of what is.

WILDWOOD LAKE

Spring dampens the land and the wind.
We climb down boulders near the water's edge.
We cast out our fishing lines and open our books.

Through books, I can feel the kindness in people.
Sometimes I imagine this kindness as God.
Since he doesn't believe in God, I try to imagine
other things the kindness could mean.
I search always for evidence of love
between characters who love each other.

Near the water, I am heightened by his eyes on me.
He likes my hair when the wind has moved it.
He likes to say my name
and then not say anything else.

A N X I E T Y

At work J tells me
the night after we went fishing
his friends threw a party at his house.
When his girlfriend arrived, she was angry.
She demanded to know where he had been all day.
She was so loud, people started to leave.

He lives by a rule:
When people ask him questions,
he doesn't lie.
So he told her he took me fishing.
She was furious.
She yelled and cried.
He told her that he and I
are just friends, that she
has nothing to worry about.

My stomach twists.
I want him to tell her something different
but I can't bring myself to say it.

I wonder what it feels like
between him and his girlfriend.
I wonder why she is dating him.
I wonder why he is dating her.
I worry that if I were dating him
he would treat me
the same way he treats her.

SOUL MATES

Here is something else he says.
He says it because he thinks it —
I'm almost sure
he has no other intentions.

He says
he doesn't believe in soul mates

but if he did
I
would be
his.

He values logic above all else.
He keeps the categories in his mind so solid.
He uses words so cleverly.

These are
some things
I like best
about him.

He plays a mean game
of hangman.

THE SILENCE CONTINUES

The soul mate comment upsets me.
I tell him he can't say things like that
because I feel the same way.
I don't know if I can work with him.
I refuse to go with him to lunch.
We work on projects in separate rooms.
In the hallways, his eyes evade mine.
Things feel awful.
Lunch is not fun alone.
I relent.
This is work, after all.
We have to be able to get along.

He asks me if I feel jealous.
The answer to this question scares me
so I shake my head *no*.
I say a different truth that is not an answer.
I tell him I want him to choose for himself
the person he wants to be with.

He says he loves talking to me.
He says he cares about me.
He says if he ever hurts me,
he will feel the worst.

We apologize to each other.
We feel lucky. We agree
that no matter what happens
we will always be friends.

GRASSLAND

Then summer comes and time reclines.
I let things between us
be whatever they want to be.
In his car I ride passenger side
sandals kicked off, legs crossed
shoulders resting in Jeff Tweedy's voice
while cigarette smoke breaks
against the air conditioner
and ashes trail on the leg of his jeans.
The world glows and swelters.
All the trees wave their arms.

Sometimes he drives us out to prairies.
Grasses, the most delicate botany,
sway in damp inclines in the wind.
Tiny flowers brush us.
We hike into the center of everything.
We wander.
The land rolls.

One evening we choose a meadow.
He walks too far ahead of me to talk.
Fireflies signal a code of peace.
We appear separate but remain together.

Later, we grow tired.
We sit down and the prairie hides us.
We think about the wind's constant motion
and the spaces plants take.

Out there, the chaos of grasses feels
so like the chaos of spirit
I wonder if my body
will be needed at all.

AT WORK

We have moved into the same cubicle.
We do every project together.
We eat every lunch together.

When we are alone in the last row of shelves
I have to remind myself
that he has a girlfriend.

When we spend all afternoon
listening to love songs
I tell myself they are not about us.

When he plasters the table in labels
printed with my name, I say to myself
that it means very little.

Still, I cannot deny that these days feel enchanted.
When the weather is nice, he takes me to the park
and we make the lunch break into a picnic.

I pack my own lunch.
His girlfriend packs his.
He says he tells her she shouldn't

but she insists.
He says he wouldn't do the same for her
unless she really needed it.

He gets upset when the lettuce
on his sandwich has brown edges.
He told her he doesn't like brown edges.

I take a deep breath. I tilt my head up
to the trees, to the green leaves,
the blue sky beyond.

I summon as much patience as I can.
I turn back to meet his gaze. I say,
brown edges are not that big of a deal.

PERSEID METEOR SHOWERS, MID-AUGUST

He calls me around midnight
because he knows I am going out
to watch the stars fall.

We draw close to the edge of a lake.
On a flat spot of land, we lay down a blanket.
The lake is a dark mirror dotted
by orange lights that shine far away.
Clouds mute the sky.
Mist is everywhere.
The line where land meets water
wobbles.

We cover ourselves with another blanket.
The space between us collapses.
Our heads touch on a pillow.

Tonight, he breathes in my ear,
is the perfect night
to lose your virginity.

I know what he means.
I know existence is closing its circle around us.
I know we are living in some type of fire.

But not even the stars, not even this fire, is enough.
Not with the girlfriend out there in the dark, waiting.
Not when all of it would mean nothing.

We lie there together for a long time.

We have no way to see
any stars come down.

D E N I A L

I didn't want to write this
but I must.

Somewhere in here
around this time
I hear a whisper.
It says
you are going to
lose him

and after you lose him
you won't want him
anymore.

I ignore this.

I think of the way his head twists when he hears something interesting,
the way his shoulders make a horizon,
the way he stands smoking with one knee bent,

and I refuse to imagine
what it would take
to not want
him.

FOR THE RECORD

We have been acting so good.
We have kept our hands off each other this whole time

but now cold weather grates on me, and my self-control slips.
Things between him and his girlfriend lurch.
I consider the probability of joy for each of us.
I decide whatever I feel for him now
I will feel regardless of sex.
I decide I would rather have him than religion.
I ask if he still thinks we should.
He says we should if I want to.

I said no before.
But now I say yes.
Yes please.
Please.

Because life is short

and we are both pretty now
and young now

and I

am hungry.

S E X   C H A N G E S   E V E R Y T H I N G   A N D   N O T H I N G

Even after I decide
I linger for a few months without action.

He never encourages me.
He asks to make sure I'm ok.
We do mostly the same things we were doing before
except now sometimes we take off some of our clothes.

His eyes gaze at me the same way they gaze at art.
His hands are just as sure as I remembered.

We create each other's bodies.
We describe our minds.

Sometimes I do everything I want to do to him.
Sometimes I save things for later.

DOG DAYS

Summer comes for us again.
Days lie down and yawn.
At lunchtime I grow languid in his armchair
while his hands shuffle chips on his plate.
A sultry wind twists through the trees.
The best type of sunlight falls at my feet.
Restlessness pulls him to the stereo
but the ideal music eludes us.
We drift into the river of afternoon
and examine each other loosely.
Let's take a nap, he says, and I nod.
He curls beside me on the bed, and we tuck
in our heads against the day's brilliance.
A single hand unclasps my bra.
I have one finger and then a second
between his jeans and his waist.
Shirts and pants slip away.
When the current washes us up,
we are thirsty. He picks up a cup and pours
the old water on a plant growing in a glass vase.
The vase is green and keeps the shape of a swan.
Its color is the color ahead of us.

MARIJUANA AND THE MODERN WORLD

J gets high so he can assign his mind to specific categories.

I get high so the stories things tell will grow louder.

Stories allow categories to contain them for a while, then spill out.

Marijuana adorns herself in crystals.

She is pleased to be the favorite daughter.

She lies on her stomach and arcs her feet slowly in the air.

Her perfume is rotting juniper, and she knows we like it.

I check to make sure being high is not what I love most.

I check to make sure I feel for him something different

than what I feel from being high.

I wish I could check the same things inside of him.

He says the things he does now don't really matter.

He says his life has not started yet because he is young.

I am not sure these statements are true.

I tell him logic can be built backwards from almost any conclusion.

He tells me logic is the foundation of the modern world.

A POSSIBILITY

I stop working with him
and the amount of time I am alone stretches.

I can recall the shape of his hands
but I can't recall the color of his eyes.
When I see him, I forget to look.

Sometimes we arrange rules for sex and then play on them.
Sometimes we pretend we are only resting.
Sometimes I know he is refusing to catch my eyes.
Sometimes I decide in advance that he has to touch me first.
Sometimes I can let him leave without touching him.

I give him a book by Denis Johnson called *Jesus Son.*
There is a line in that book that goes
we were so in love we didn't know what it was

A DECISION

He keeps no girlfriends but he sleeps with other girls.
He tells me about some of them.

I nod.
I hesitate.
I see the world as if from under water.
I mostly stop talking about him to my friends
because I find no one who understands.
I consider not seeing him anymore.
But then I think, if we ever had anything between us to lose

it is now irretrievable.

So I carry on.

WHITE EARTH LAKE, MINNESOTA

That summer I take him with me on vacation.
Sometime after, these lines appear:

The lake prefers stillness.
We lounge in canoes and drape our arms down.

We cause the smallest ripples.
The sun illuminates radiant green depths.

Sometime between dark and dawn,
fog takes the space where water and air collide.

It shifts and grows frustrated.
It speaks the way he speaks.

Far away, a loon whimpers.
The stillness doesn't break

It rises.

A SECRET

He stands not quite ready in the doorway
and reaches out his arms so that I will step into them.
I follow him into the bedroom and perch behind him.
The mirror frames both of us in harsh evening light.

He arches his back to pull on jeans.
He pushes his hair into familiar tapers.
His glance falls into mine
and something moves through his face.

I bite back words about how beautiful he is
because he doesn't seem like he wants me to say them.

CAGED LOVE IS NOT LOVE

I feel for him as I feel for the sparrows.
I want them to have the whole forest,
to perch in the branches they like best,
to sing the songs born in them to sing.

In his car, sad music pours from the radio.
We are young, he says. *We should use this time*
to experiment, to see who we can love
and who we cannot.

If only another boy would come my way.
If only I could imagine a different
pair of hands on my stomach,
a different mouth biting.

Through the car windows,
brown fields stretch,
and over them combines churn.

If I were to speak, tears would spill with my words.
If I were to cry, the other girls would remain.

He pulls the car to the curb in front of my place.
I look into his eyes and promise myself
this time I will not forget their color,
the color of seeds and harvest, of dying leaves.

Yes, sparrows come and go as they please.
So does the wind.
So does anything free.

I AM AFRAID SOMETHING IS WRONG

Religion was a harbor that I turned my back on.

I used to believe I could create a joyful world through my actions,

that God held rewards and intended some for me.

Maybe my joy has fled because my actions have driven it out.

I scrounge for answers, but none hold up under the light.

I commit myself again to kneel in the temple of my heart.

In the books, life eventually breaks people down.

The nonessential shatters, and we are left only with the real.

In order to have something to grasp, we are required to acknowledge love.

But my life is not a book.

And I cannot make another person love me.

I am afraid that either something is wrong with his heart

or something is wrong with mine.

ANDREW BIRD PLAYS THE SOKOL UNDERGROUND

It was anything but hear the voice
That says that we're all basically alone
— Andrew Bird

It is spring. The evening is damp and electric.
A line of dark clouds hovers on the horizon.

I put on a skirt with pleats like a schoolgirl's.
I zip my cardigan all the way up.

When we arrive, the phonographs are already spinning.
Andrew Bird and his violin chase the truth around.

J says he believes it too: each of us is alone on this earth.
But I don't believe it. I can't.

In the scarred bathroom mirror, I see sadness in my own eyes.
But then I blink, and the marijuana makes everything look pretty.

Later, I watch him disappear into his apartment.
Fat drops of rain plop on the windshield.

I circle the block.
I gaze at the face of my phone.

I call.
I crawl into his bedroom.

I lean against the bed and begin peeling off my clothes,
slowly, slowly. The damp pieces sticking to my skin.

He catches me there, says, *No. What are you doing? Wait.*
So I wait. In the orange glow of the streetlamp

he rubs me as if to keep me warm. My shoulders
my stomach, my thighs with the skirt still over them.

Rain pounds on the windows.
Thunder and lightning ravage the scene outside.

When we are done, he reaches out and takes my hand.
All my fingers with his fingers.
The rain relentless.

2

What started in winter and became summer
turned to winter again.
A long winter.
Years of winter.

I tell myself I should have known.
Nothing lovely lasts.

A TERRIBLE CHANCE

When will he leave?
He will leave in early fall, for environmental law school
where he will learn to manipulate rules for the greater good.
He will write categories to help the prairies that we've loved.
He will take his new girlfriend with him.
He says he wants to be serious about her
because they think a lot alike.
When he leaves it will still be warm outside
and everyone will be soaking it up
because everyone knows the warm won't last.

When will he leave?
He won't leave. He can't.
He won't be able to leave me.

I consider the terrible chance
that he's never been here at all.

FARMLAND

That late summer the center of me contorts.
I ache for enough release to let something wild run through me.

A relentless sun throbs on the horizon.
Dust from gravel roads dirties the houses we used to gaze at.

Each time we walked this land, I felt an inch of me root down.
I could have sworn some part of him took hold too.

We don't talk about time anymore.
The light in his eyes dims.

If a crop quits in the fields, if rain prefers the sky,
who among us can say otherwise?

Here is the blunt truth of things:
One day he is gone.
He does not say goodbye.
He does not call.

Now wind searches the parched fields.
Now distant trees shudder.

THE WORLD HAS RULES AFTER ALL AND THEY ARE CRUEL

The blade of loneliness is whet so thin
you can't watch it go in.

I open my mouth to tell him something
but of course he isn't here.

The words in my mind writhe.

I keep standing up to find the ceiling lowered.
I hit my head in the exact same place each time.

DARKNESS OBSCURES
EVERYTHING

The past weighs heavy in my hands as I raise it.
I grope for flaws, for the parts of us that built this ruin.

I wanted him to recognize the same joy in himself that I did.
I wanted the intensity of desire to drive him to words.
I wanted a space made in my own shape to open next to him.
Somehow I wanted something wrong.

My stomach is sick and I need to lie down.
I close my eyes for a very long time.

WHAT THE WORLD REQUIRES

I follow the season down, fearing the worst still lies ahead.
The light in me is like the light in the sky: each day a little less.
I feel constrained to a space the size of a bathtub.
I watch movies. I drink.
When I feel capable of using words, I see friends.
In the evenings, I dull my mind with walking.

The homes in the neighborhoods blink sleepily with love.
In front of one, children throw a football and shriek commands.
Around the yard lurks a thicket of vines and thorns, all tangled and hunched.
A mother sits near the vines, as if warning them to keep back.
She glances up, and her face contains all the fragility one person can stand.

Love, no matter what happens, promise me you won't be sad.
The world permits strange vines.
It requires them.

THE INTERSECTION

Religion has evaporated, but the possibility of God floats like high clouds.

I know the way to become a person who can't get out of bed in the morning

is to not get out of bed in the morning. So I force myself to rise each day.

I offer myself bribes. In exchange for a cigarette,

I climb into my car and face the intersection that leads to work.

Even when no cars pass, the lights change anyway.

Someone paced the intervals between lights.

Someone appears on schedule to change the bulbs.

If God has a brain, there is a ticking in it, and the lights turn on the

same pattern.

I am afraid that all the lights in the world form constellations,

and that I am the only person who sees them.

When he was here, he helped me chart constellations, saw shapes I didn't.

Each day the ticking in God's brain magnifies.

The whole world is built of concrete and metal and gasoline and paint.

THE SCENT OF WATER

Gratitude for the time work takes.

Gratitude for a way to exhaust my strength.

At lunch in the garden, a familiar, nameless smell startles me.

Even though the nights are cold now, the days are still hot.

I sweat. What appears inside me might not be true.

What I can remember about feeling good,

I remember so slowly I could have pulled it from a dream.

At home the space by the sink fills up with empty glasses,

though I'm almost certain I don't drink much of anything at all.

Maybe I have been alone too much.

I open all the windows to invite something in,

but nothing comes. I try to be patient.

I try to hold still in what I know about the heart:

mostly that change, as it comes, cannot be seen.

After a while the room, the night, the world itself,

appear only in shades of gray and white.

I raise my head, but the air holds a smell like nothing,

like the scent of water.

NOTHING IS OKAY BY THE EVERYBODYFIELDS

From law school J tosses me scraps.
He is sorry for not saying goodbye.
He feels bad.
He misses me.

I refuse to beg.
I reciprocate a casual tone.

He suggests I listen to new music he has found.
He says some of the songs remind him
of me.

I wait for dusk.
I lie on the living room floor
watch the last streaks of sun trace over the walls
and listen.

Folk music with chords as sad as a mountain river.
Lyrics about fields with no crops, boys
who leave home, young people who fuck
each other up. A banjo and a fiddle.

Yes, the floor I can lie on.
The floor I can understand.

LINES I COLLECT IN MY JOURNAL

From Charles Bukowski
(the title of the first book J gave to me):
Love Is a Dog from Hell

From Muriel Rukeyser:
I remember the girls laughing
I remember they said he only wanted to get away from me
I remember mother saying: inventors are like poets,
a trashy lot
I remember she told me those who try out inventions are worse
I remember she added: Women who love such are the
Worst of all

From Linda Gregg:
I always thought joy was the way
we were supposed to feel, was the ordinary,
and that everything else was strange.
I believe that being requires the other, and the sacred
requires the thing. But I am alone. I must discover
my heart against rock. If you do this to me, if you
do this to me, if you take your love away, if you take,
if you go away, you will make my heart blind in me.

From Eleanor Lerman:
I set a chair beside the pool
but cannot occupy its space. Cannot. Which is why I followed
you: to learn how to enter the world.

From James Wright:

We are not exhausted. We are not angry, or lonely,
or sick at heart.
We are in love lightly, lightly. We know we are shining,
though we cannot see one another.

From Frank X. Gaspar:

You don't want less love — this ground has been covered before —
you want more love, even when you can't say what it means,
even though it binds you to the world which you can only lose.

From Kim Addonizio:

Love's
merciless, the way it travels in
and keeps emitting light.

THERE IS A TYPE OF SADNESS THAT PERVADES EVERYTHING

Christmas Holiday, Winnebago, Minnesota

All night the north wind tears at the yard and the house.
Boards and nails groan.
Frost freezes over frost.
Roofs and trees shoulder equal burden.

In the morning, coffee and a restless spirit.
I take the dogs to the edge of town and set them loose.
Their slobbering, wagging joy cracks again
the shell of my heart so that I wish once more
what I have wished every day since he left.

For miles I follow the dogs on the slick, packed gravel.
Where else can I go?
Across the earth sweeps a deep, deep cold,
the kind that hurts the body,
but is understood only by the heart,
which knows such cold in other forms.
This is what I mean when I tell my friend Christine
we cannot run away from ourselves.
We can only run away from places,
and places look like the inside of us.

I turn back, finally, and the clouds split.
Sunlight gleams on the tundra.
I wince in the brilliance and turn my eyes down.
There in the road lies a silence so heavy
I wish my heart wouldn't beat so loudly.

I know I will stand there until the cold grows unbearable.
I know I will call the dogs and trudge back home.
I know what delirium has risen will vanish for a while, then return.
I know the snow will remain for many more days.

ADDITIONS TO THE RECORD

He comes back for vacation and calls me.
He misses seeing my face.
He wishes we could talk more often.
Sometimes he dreams about me.

I refuse to have sex with him
unless he agrees to tell the other girl.
I spread blankets for him to sleep on the couch.

By morning I have weakened.
I let him into my bedroom.

His eyes search mine.
My smile feels tight.
But even this placebo
makes me grateful.

I have been sick since he left.
I cried every day for a few months.
I threw up occasionally.

I cry less now.

I never cry in front of him.

I want him to ask me to be his.
I want him to choose on his own.
I want him
to be happy.

Love is the dungeon
from which I cannot
desire to free myself.

NOTES FROM WINTER THAT REMAIN UNSENT

.

1: It's Not Too Late to Fix This

Buy a plane ticket with some of that loan money.
Call me on repeat until I answer.
Shove me against a wall.
Say you were crazy to leave, and you'll never do it again.
The second you wake up, the second you are ready
come fucking get me.

2: Sometimes I Catch Myself Wishing You Pain

Winter still.
Long rows of torn corn.
This same cold must chill you too.
It must.

3: I Have Been Thinking of You Slightly Less Frequently

Alone again at dawn, I beg the world to send me a sign.
How long will you be away before I can think of you
as gone?

MOONLIGHT

There is a fine line between being brave and being stupid,
and I have no idea on which side of that line he falls.
When I met him, a part of me held paralyzed stood up and shivered.
He never really asked to call, and mostly he didn't,
but when he did, he wanted me: the inner part that matters.
His words held ideas of me that were true,
and he came closer to me than anyone else ever.
When he listened to me, his eyes glimmered with recognition,
and even in silence, understanding moved like a river between us.
He did not kiss me often, but sometimes he stared into my eyes
in such a way that I almost could not remain standing.
Once, after, when we were still lying in bed, he held my hand.
But now he is gone, and I am just alone. Always alone.
Alone though the world holds a hundred million things,
though I have a lot of friends and sometimes other men.
Other men who are more kind, who ask to call and do.
But if I fuck them, I feel only one type of pleasure,
and in the night, if I sleep, I am truly asleep.
Even in the privacy of my own mind,
I am ashamed to use the word *love*.
But also I am ashamed not to use it.
There is nothing to be done either way.
I must wait to see how things want to be,
if they want to be any way at all.
This, I realize, is how planets feel around the sun.
Then, worse, how the earth keeps the dark side of the moon.

A GIRL'S STORY

The fairy tales are lies of the highest order.
Love does not look like a princess
in a pretty dress
with pretty hair.

Love looks bloody and wild.
It looks like a horse tearing through
a barbed wire fence.

MAYBE I HAVE READ
TOO MANY STORIES

Did this happen because I imagine too hard?

Because I want to make real what I have read?

Because the love that interests me overpowers the people it comes for?

Because the best stories prize wild hearts?

Because the wild hearts make me feel alive?

Did this begin during that time when I talked only to my cat?

The time when I climbed every tree that would let me?

Did this happen because the trees nod with such kindness?

Because the pulse in each tree matched my own?

THE SICKNESS

I want his eyes to pin me to the wall the way they used to.
I want him to put his mouth over mine the way he did before.

I want to make him smoke a cigarette and watch
while I take off all my clothes.
I want to tie his hands to the back of a chair.
I want. I want.
I must not
want.

He writes to ask me
if I would I like to have a last engagement
when he comes home on break.
Since he plans to be with his girlfriend forever.
Since we deserve a proper goodbye.

Would I like to?
Would I like these fantasies made real?
No.
I would like to
but I can't.

He says
tell me about the fantasies.

No.

Tell me.

I tell a little.
A chair, I say. *Black lace. A cigarette indoors.*

We must, he says.
We can help each other end this.

Then tell her. So she knows.
So she can choose.

But he will not tell her unless she asks.

The sickness returns then, stronger than ever.
An ache through my whole body.
He would take the best things and twist them
until nothing lovely remains.
He would put his body next to mine
as a way of saying goodbye.
Can't he see that my body
refuses to say goodbye?
That I can only say *stay*.
Stay and *stay.*

AFTER BUKOWSKI, PART 1

Bukowski, you were right.

Reasons to hate this life multiply.
The world makes the heart look stupid.
People act ugly toward each other.
The bottom of the gut aches.

For years now, I've loved a boy
who's been fucking lots of other women
and doing lots of other shitty things.
He is trying to be like you.

I feel ashamed.
I feel so alone.

Sometimes I think the days
are like a boy who brings me gifts
but never says anything interesting.

I try to believe I won't always
feel this way.

My days are gleeful, Bukowski.
They are running away from me
like wild horses over the hills
exactly the way you promised.

AFTER BUKOWSKI, PART 2

Old men who remind me of you
stand on street corners
smoking in the relief of a thaw.
I know they watch me.
I care very little.

I hear a voice that I imagine
sounds like yours.
It says *someday*
on a day
that won't feel much different
than today,
you will be 80.

Likewise,
on another
similar day
you will die.

Bukowski,
each one of us
is a dirty old man
on a street corner.

Each of us
has two
cigarettes
and we are smoking,
smoking.

3

In every discipline
certain aspects
grow in proportion,
take on
light.

NOTES TO MYSELF

Don't be afraid.
You will never know everything.
You will never fix everything.
Expect pain.
Expect fumbling.
Try to observe everything without anger.
Maybe someday someone will see this as courage.
Maybe someday you will see it as courage, too.

So no light shines on the attic stairs.
Reach out your hands and climb anyway.
Feel for the door frame and step out on any board that will hold.
If you arrive intact on the highest balcony, stand on the railing.
The sky owns the stars, but they swing low
over the edge of the earth.
What falls from above them
falls also on you.

WIND SHAKES THE TREES

and rain throws herself down.
They shriek and argue all night.

In the morning, I wish I could
have disappeared with them.

Shredded branches litter streets and sidewalks.
I can't blame the trees for this mess
but I can't blame the wind either.

Arms made of branches.
Arms that reach always toward wind and sky,
though wind and sky are not always kind.

There are some truths I need to set down for a while.
There are some truths my mind has no place to put.

Maybe now he stands on a porch and smokes a cigarette.
Maybe he studies a line of trees that have stood for a hundred years.
Maybe the sky is mostly gray with a single orange line on fire.

The mind is magic. It moves like fish in water.
The mind touches the infinite but lives in space and time.
Even in sleep the mind swims the banks of the river that holds it,
examining the shore.

I open the windows to a world that smells like worms.

Between the worms, tree roots creep.

They drink whatever water they find.

If some of the water is dirty

some of the leaves will go brilliant and fall away.

SOMETHING WE HAVEN'T FOUND THE END OF

At work I look out through a large window.

Traffic careens down the street.

Everything moves except me.

I wonder when something new will enter.

I wonder if anything coming is coming for me.

At times the sitting and watching seem like a new kind of low.

But other times pigeons rise on bursts of wind,

and I find myself astonished to see how far up the sky goes.

God was a plan that failed long ago,

but there is something infinite, I think.

Or at least there's something we haven't found the end of.

So I stay sitting.

The traffic rotates through the city.

The variations are real but insignificant.

THE SOUND

It is summer. J wants me for an evening.
I trace my way on the old roads to his parents' house.
Gravel and sunset. Gnats in the tassels of corn.

He meets me in the yard where fireflies are just
appearing. The wind rustles. Crickets chirp.
Dusk sneaks in, damp and chilly.

We return to Wildwood Lake, where we used to fish.
A full moon shows me his face but hides his eyes.
We drink a little beer and remember each other.

We see no other people.
We take off our clothes and slip into the lake.
The frogs and cicadas drum.
The water smells like mold.

When we climb out, we have one blanket
to share as a towel. He gets pissed because
I still have my underwear on.
He says it's not fair.

I remind him about his girlfriend.

We move to a different spot.
I take off all my clothes.
To be fair.
This time I wade in from a landing.
I don't stand close to him.

Afterward, the car heater hums.
Country music plays on the radio.
From home, a hot shower beckons.

I drive him to his brother's house.
If he were to ask, I would break.
I would take him home with me.

But he doesn't, and I don't.

My breath draws in as if to speak.
The words line up in my mind.
My mouth opens.
But the sound stays inside.
The sound goes around.

FURNITURE

I sit alone in my apartment with the walls solid around me.
My foot rests on a table I could kick if I wanted to.
A foot that can feel pain.

To him, nothing matters.
He doesn't need anything permanent.
But I do.
I need to know the chairs will hold when I sit on them.
I need to feel myself sitting and afterwards
remember it was real.

So I will sit then, with all my power.
I will be an end table or a lamp.
Anything, however small.
Anything with all my fucking realness.

EVERY COIN HAS TWO SIDES

1:

I feel I have been playing a game
with a person who turns out to be imaginary.
Except maybe he never said he wasn't imaginary
and maybe I chose not to ask.

2:

Maybe all feeling is the thing to lose.
Maybe my type of desire doesn't work in this world.
I have been acting like I'm ok for so long,
I don't even know how to say I'm not ok.
And even if I say I'm not ok,
what could possibly be done now?
I remember that in old stories,
explorers never feel diminished for being alone.
They are men mostly, and even as children,
they were told to expect isolation.
They do not let sadness creep into them.

A DROP OF SANITY

I know I need to talk about this.
I know girls who are good at talking.

They say *he sounds like an asshole.*
Clearly, he doesn't love you.

Asshole? That's not the half of it.
Doesn't love me? Are you sure?
Have you been watching?
Have you been listening?
Have you been paying attention?

What should I do about my heart?

You need to go out. You need
to forget about this for a while.

Where should I go? How
will I forget? I am so
confused. Love is failing.
Language is failing. I
am failing.

Maegan, my married friend,
is confused, too. But she loves me.
She wants to help. Finally she says
I guess I am lucky.
I guess it's the best thing
that the person I love
loves me back.

Thank you thank you thank you thank you.
A drop of sanity.
I am a cactus a bacteria a pond scum.
I can live off this drop
for years.

MORE LINES I COLLECT
IN MY JOURNAL

From Natalie Portman in *Closer*:
This is not a war.

From Tony Hoagland:
by now you were beginning to suspect
that everyone
lived a secret life
of acts they never advertised
and you were right

From Chris Beckett:
I wait for you to appear
after the years
and take me fishing: somewhere tonight
you are sitting again on the sand
of my thoughts
untying your shoes

From Mary Kate McCarney:
the decade lost
in velveteen hills
mother said: imagination
when deep enough
becomes a kind of sorcery

From Cormac McCarthy:

What he loved in horses was what he loved in men,
the blood and the heat of the blood that ran them.
All his reverence and all his fondness and all the leanings of his life
were for the ardenthearted
and they always would be so and would never be
otherwise.

From Abraham Lincoln:

I desire so to conduct the affairs of this administration that if at the end...
I have lost every other friend on earth,
I shall at least have one friend left, and that friend
shall be down inside of me.

GEOLOGY

I make my phone into a fence I lie against,
my back to the posts, dug in.
I wait.
The fence cuts through a familiar field.
Moonlight throws harsh shadows.
Only breezes touch me.

When I look into the future,
I see weather and water on land.
I see ground rise and fall away,
the field turned in on itself,
thin rivers spreading new soil
over the whole place until
the earth takes a new shape.

Yes, if a shift is to come,
it will come so slowly
everything here will be unrecognizable.
I will be in a different age entirely.

THE WAY THE WORLD WAS

In the beginning the earth was a molten mass of iron.
Everything before and since has been expanding.

Always, we contract in patterns within the larger expansion.
Our motions make math and art.

The place near my esophagus where I miss him most
was made billions of years ago.
You could prove this in an equation.

Between him and me there is mostly silence now.
The way the world was before life crept from the waters.

Though, of course, there were wind and rain.
And the sounds of land calling for plants.

E R O S I O N

He returns from law school with a mind
tightened to almost breaking.

He has no money.
He has no idea where he'll find a job
or how much time finding a job will take.

He breaks up with his girlfriend but
they keep living in the same house.

He and I go out to bars. We see music shows.
When she is away, he and I return
in darkness to sleep in their bed.

Pictures of them line the mantel.
In the bathroom, all the soaps are scented.

I feel how much she wants him
and her sickness is my sickness.

In the morning he makes me breakfast.
When I leave, the summer sky is burdened with clouds.

In my car mirror I barely recognize myself.
I put on music I used to love, but all the love is gone.

I didn't know things could feel this bad.
The line blurred into almost nothing.
The meaning worn down
too low for words.

HOW LIFE IS MADE

Time has not made him better.
Time has made him worse.

I feel the way people do
when they add money on a bad bet.

He moves into a building two blocks from mine.
Girls come and go from his bedroom.

He tells me about some of them:
girls who work behind counters,
girls on the internet, girls outside bars.

I listen.
I understand and
I do not understand.

He is still breaking things
and putting none of them back together.
He still insists that nothing counts.

I long for someone
to come and rescue me.

But no one is coming.

My mind begs for someone to be here,
tries to see who is here, exactly.

My heart, having known all along, says,
make something of this.
Of this, make your whole life.

And me wanting to make a life.
And me unsure how life is made.

DESPITE EVERYTHING,
I WANT TO UNDERSTAND

I wonder if he feels anything for me at all.
I wonder if he wants something I don't have.
Maybe I am not pretty enough or
smart enough or rich enough.
I wonder if he lives off something
between him and the other girls
that I can't comprehend.
Worst, I wonder if he has simply decided
to never let a feeling matter.

I know he chases accomplishment,
but I wonder what happens once some things
are accomplished?
I wonder what the point is
of doing kind things outwardly
but being unkind
to the people
close to you.

I admit that he may know more
than me. I admit that my own
approach to life
seems like a poor one.

REALITY

The world my heart wants to live in isn't real.
The man in that world
talks down to girls,
cheats, deceives, manipulates,
wears cologne that smells so good
it hurts your heart.

There is no space for me in that world.
He has filled it all with himself.

4

Nothing is safe
from the hands of time.

WHAT HAPPENS

I break, finally.
I am always the one
who breaks.
I say *J, for God's sake*
I love you.
I love you and
I can't ask you to change
but if you do change
you must tell me.
Promise me
you will tell me
if you love me
enough to try.

He gives his word *yes.*
He promises.
We lie back against my couch.
We rest in the peace of agreement.

Later, in February, one week brings days that are almost hot.
All the snow melts except these tiny fingers of dirty drifts
that linger in crevices blocked from the wind and sun.

We seize the warmest day.
He drives me to a prairie we have not visited before.
We hike through grasses until we lose the road,
and we spread a blanket on a hillside.
We take off all our clothes.

Later, we put all our clothes back on.
We go home.

Sex is not love.
Sex is not love.
Sex is not even closeness.
Sex is one body
accommodating another.

A SIGN

A few weeks later he finds a job.
He rents a farmhouse that looks out on fields.

I give an afternoon to help him move
though I know he would not do the same for me.

I am tired of keeping score.
I am just plain tired.

The drive takes hours that feel outside of time.
We listen to NPR and smoke like we used to.

I wonder if I will ever ride with him again.
I gaze out at the dead plants and dirt, hoping for a sign.

The heat in the farmhouse is turned way down.
Snow obscures the road on our way home.

In front of my house he leans back into the seat.
He does not step out to hug me goodbye.

He does say thank you, I think.
His eyes retreat.

I shroud myself in silence.
A year or so passes.

When I learn that he is engaged,
I am with my new boyfriend.

I wait until my boyfriend leaves
to cry.

REMAINS

Heart, what do you want from me?
I have followed you everywhere.
I have permitted you everything,

because life dulls,
the world fades
without the heart.

But you insist on pain.
You shame me at every turn.

I played my best game.
I failed.

If you want something else, tell me.
Take whatever you will.

What do I have left to lose?
What do I have left to fear?

STILL MORE LINES I COLLECT

From Russ Semm's answering machine:
This is not an answering machine
rather, this is a questioning machine
and the question is who are you
and what are you doing here?

Many things from David Foster Wallace, but especially this:
The truth will set you free
but not until it's finished with you.

From Tataya's Yoga Class:
After all, how can you expect other people
to be real, if you aren't real?

From the Bhagavad Gītā:
By cherishing each other
you shall attain the highest welfare.

From Thomas's Yoga Class:
The question is not, "Can you do this?"
The question is, "Can you do this
with a little bit of grace?"

CEREMONIES

I am so grateful I made him promise.
I am so grateful I told him how I feel.

I don't know if he ever loved me.
I don't know if he is capable of the kind of love I want.

But I know the time has come.

This story requires a sacrifice
and no one else can give it.

I learned these rules in books.
I doubt them now, but I have nothing else to follow.

So I stay awake far into the night.
The stars pretend they aren't withdrawing.

The blade of time glistens.
I put out a hand and pick it up.

I cut out my desire for him.

I cut out the part of me that needs him
to love me back in order to make my love real.

I conduct the ceremonies myself.
I am the only audience.

Priestess.

Witch.

Slut.

Whatever.

What do words matter anyway?

WHAT A DANGEROUS PLACE
THE MIND CAN BE

The thoughts in my head have been saying
my story needs to be the perfect story.

Saying my way of loving should never hurt.

Saying failure means I am wrong at my core.

Saying if he breaks me, I will crack forever.

My thoughts
have been hunting me.

Let them feast.

THINGS I LAY DOWN

So I was abandoned.
So I gave everything I knew how to give
for love that was not returned.

Those are some things about me.
Those are some things that bite.

I leave those things here because
I lack the strength to carry them anymore.

I deny the beast in my mind any more power.
I watch the thoughts with teeth pass.

I don't want to hate him.
I can't hate him.
I love him.

I lay down my anger
because it makes me resent him
for his lack of courage.

I lay down my fear
because it keeps me pinned
and I need to move.

I lay down my sadness because
it doesn't make me feel good
and I haven't felt good in so long.

W I T H O U T   H I M   I   D R I F T

and I do not mind.

I want to live in the desert.
I want to dance on old rocks.
I want to fuck blond men with dirty hair.
Just kidding.
Don't get any ideas.
I don't want anything.

I want to live in this stillness forever.

From emptiness truth rises.
Words knock.

Never again will I harbor shame
about the things that I love.

Never again will I not speak the cold truth
in the moment that I know it.

My heart may have caused me pain
but I will pick it anyway.

I won't look down on myself when
the path I choose disappears.

WHAT I CAN MAKE OF THIS

I am an electron
summoned
by a stronger
valence.

I was a barrier
and I got
dissolved.

Here is the pure gold coin.
I have polished it
and now it glows.
The face on this coin smiles.

I was brave
but I could have
been
braver.

No matter
now.

Peace is a place
I can make.

FINALLY, FOR THE RECORD

He knows.
I tell him.
I send him these poems.
I tell him I don't love him
that way anymore.

He says he didn't know.
He didn't know I
could ever love him.
He didn't trust himself.
He cared for me too much
to make me something that could
disappear.

He needed me
to be his friend.

He gives permission
for you to read this.

He likes the poems
when he pretends
they aren't about him.

He says he is proud of me.
He says the truth helps.

We agree to be friends.
We agree to call this
art.

GIRLS AND BOYS

1.

The girls try to hide the sadness
in their eyes. They arrange their hair
and smooth their makeup.
They are happiest when people
treat them like they are pretty.
But they are starting to wonder
if they aren't pretty enough
because no one has been
caring about them,
no one has been
treating them
like they are pretty.

2.

The boys are frustrated.
So many girls look pretty.
The boys want to watch,
they want to touch,
they want to be around.
Sometimes the boys
play the girls like a game.
Sometimes the girls play the boys.
Sometimes everyone shifts
in and out of
being real.

THE GARDEN

If you want to walk in the goddamn garden
you better be sure you find the garden you want to walk in

because believe me you will walk.

And later,

did this happen because no one mentioned
we are supposed to be making a garden?

Did we forget that we must build beauty?

Who is taking care of the plants?

What are we going to eat?

And, later still,

I will address this heart problem.

He will care for the land and the air.

I know the garden
has more than one entrance.

DAVID FOSTER WALLACE

Before he hanged himself
he said he was going to communicate
what it felt like to be a fucking human being
or die trying.

He also said this:

> "Her silhouette leans
> and says
>> 'And Lo, for the Earth was empty of form, and void.
>> 'And Darkness was all over the Face of the Deep.
>> 'And We said:
>> 'Look at that fucker *Dance.*'"

LOVE

This is the way things always begin:
Something invites you to enter a story.
When you enter, you do so
without knowing the end.
If you want to know, you must stay with your heart.
You must not turn away
even when forced to look upon yourself.
If you never look, your story will pass unknown.
This culture is a shell.
The religions, just shells.
Even the poems, you see.
Love is all there is.
Love is all there is and
love wants you.
Love wants your mind
to examine
to recognize
to delight.
Love sprang up through the atoms and the dust
through the light and the rocks and the plants
through the fish and the elephants
to find you
to meet you
here, now.
Love wants to be known
wants you
to be the home
it inhabits.

This is how you know love:
You see it.

EPILOGUE

After the teachings of zen master Linji Yïxuan

if
on any day
at any time
you see

if you see
the buddha
in
the road

drop everything

ask her
what it would take
for her to let you
run her over

and if she tells you
you must obey
you must give
your very best

then
if she smiles
if she nods

you

run her over
and over

run!

NOTES

A POSSIBILITY
Denis Johnson, *Jesus Son*, Farrar, Straus & Giroux, 1992

LINES I COLLECT IN MY JOURNAL
Charles Bukowski, *Love Is a Dog from Hell*, Black Sparrow Press, 1977

Muriel Rukeyser, "Waiting for Icarus," originally published in *Breaking Open*, 1973

Linda Gregg, "The Terrifying Power of Darkness Is Inseparable from the Redemptive Power of the Sacred," in *Chosen by the Lion*, Graywolf Press, 1994

Eleanor Lerman, "Timeless Canyon," in *Our Post-Soviet History Unfolds*, Sarabande Books, 2005

James Wright, "Yes, But," in *About the River: The Complete Poems* (published posthumously), Farrar, Straus & Giroux, 1992

Frank X. Gaspar, "One Thousand Blossoms," in *Night of a Thousand Blossoms*, Alice James Books, 2004

Kim Addonizio, "Stolen Moments," in *What Is This Thing Called Love: Poems*, W.W. Norton, 2004

AFTER BUKOWSKI, PART 1
Charles Bukowski, *The Days Run Away Like Wild Horses Over the Hills*, Black Sparrow Press, 1969

MORE LINES I COLLECT IN MY JOURNAL

Closer, Patrick Marber (writer), Mike Nichols (director), Columbia Pictures, 2004

Tony Hoagland, "Carnal Knowledge," in *Sweet Ruin,* University of Wisconsin Press, 1992

Chris Beckett, "About the fish in Lake Langano," in *Ethiopia Boy,* Oxford Poets, 2013

Mary Kate McCarney, "Grand Junction," in *The Common Lattice* (unpublished), 2011

Cormac McCarthy, *All the Pretty Horses,* Alfred A. Knopf, 1992

Abraham Lincoln, speech to a Missouri delegation, circa 1861

STILL MORE LINES I COLLECT

David Foster Wallace, *Infinite Jest,* Little, Brown, 1996

Tataya Bailey (formerly Tataya Radtke), yoga instructor

Bhagavad-Gītā, Book 3, Section 11. Translation by Winthrop Sargeant, SUNY Press, 1984

Thomas Radtke, yoga instructor

DAVID FOSTER WALLACE

"Fiction's about what it is to be a fucking human being." In Larry McCaffery, "A Conversation with David Foster Wallace," *The Review of Contemporary Fiction,* Summer 1993, Vol. 13.2

"I will be a fiction writer again or die trying." In a letter to his agent, Bonnie Nadell (various sources)

David Foster Wallace, *Infinite Jest*, Little, Brown, 1996

EPILOGUE

The teachings of Linji Yixuan are quite old (circa 850 CE), and translations vary. But the relevant one goes something like this: "If you meet the Buddha on the road, kill him."

THANKS

Abiding gratitude to my husband, Zachary Wolff, who has never inspired a single sad love poem. To Hilda Raz, who guided my earliest years as a poet, when many of these poems were first written. To Carolyn Hunter, whose encouragement ushered this manuscript out of my old gmail account.

ABOUT THE AUTHOR

Teresa Wolff is a poet and storyteller living in the foothills of the Rocky Mountains. She's endlessly fascinated by human nature and the strange things people will do in the right (or wrong) circumstances. *All Things Sane* is her first collection of poetry and she is at work on a young adult fantasy novel. When not writing, Wolff is trying to think of something to make for dinner, tending her herd of children, or moving her perennials for the millionth time.

www.ingramcontent.com/pod-product-compliance
Lightning Source LLC
Chambersburg PA
CBHW030311130626
46549CB00002B/803